The Home Stretch

a cycle of poems

by

Michael Campagnoli

Published by Unsolicited Press
www.unsolicitedpress.com

Copyright © 2017 Michael Campagnoli
All Rights Reserved.

No part of this book may be reproduced or transmitted in any form or by any means without written permission from the publisher or author.

For information, contact publisher at
info@unsolicitedpress.com

Unsolicited Press Books are distributed to the trade by Ingram.
Printed in the United States of America.
ISBN: 978-1-947021-10-5

Poems

Long Shadows	2
Loons	3
Prelude	5
If We're Not A Dream We're Nothing	7
The Long Ride Home	8
Abound	9
Loons: the cycle	12
Madness	19
Wolf	23
The Home Stretch	25
The First Time He Saw Her	29
Night	30
White in the Moon the Long Road Lies	31
Mirror Image	34
Alewives	37
Ocean in the Trees	41
All Knowledge is an Act of Faith	44
Him	48
Inner Night	49
Holy Trinity	50
What she remembered...	51
The Blue Rose	53
The Remex	55

For Miss Fern Alane

The Home Stretch

Long Shadows

Before dawn,
in mirrored light but no sun,
she saw the birds leaving.
Going south. Row upon row
in strict cuneal formation.
Or raucous, in cluttered disarray.
Flying low, fading high
up in the sky.
Heading out.

Later, running past the cove
in mittens and hat,
she heard them cry far in the distance:
a nameless feeling of affection and regret.
Only the loons remained,

Old friends.
Their time would come, too.

The time of long shadows.

Loons

> Across the cove
> a woman's scream
> a peal of girlish laughter.

Loons
First time,
Never a sound before
a cry so stark it startled her;
the decibel force of it.
a pitch so high,
it took her breath away.

There, in the distance,
two threw back
their wet black heads, gave
> *answer and reply*
> *answer and reply*
> sad-sweet skirl of melody.
Almost entwined, they slipped
beneath the water's edge. Silent.
Disappeared.
Loons

The black and white geometry.
The undulating glow
of beak and neck and eye.
The haunted-peculiar call:

euphoric horn
cello of melancholy
ephemeral and doomed

Swimming. Their backs
                like
                  white
    spotted
    endless night sky.

Loons.

Prelude

out the kitchen window
movement caught her eye.

washing breakfast dishes,
movement caught her eye.

a peripheral blur,
a sudden presence
up the hill,

there, where the road escaped
the darkness of the wood,
out in the sun-bright newness
of the unfledged world:

> *this way came the stranger*
>
> down the hill he shambled,
> stocky and unkempt,
> stuffed in three sweaters
> a shabby overcoat,
> a frayed blue watch-cap on his head.

at the bottom, in the clearing,
he stopped, gave a squint,
a feral sniff of the air

            alert
            cautious,
            looked slowly,
side to side,
            then stalked
                        down the road
            with unmistakable intent,
            head thrust forward,
            a long deliberate stride,

            as if he caught the scent of prey,
            as if he came to some decision.

If We're Not A Dream We're Nothing

cold November wind
blasted to the bone
shook the branches bare—
there, where the road,
cut through the orchard

each Fall Maynard Bray
paid brown-skinned men
from far away
to pick the apples clean and leave
empty trees
        and gone

        lonely in the
vacant light

The Long Ride Home

Scaffold over-arched the road

broad-backed tall black oak and elm
a spider's web of branches
reached to seize the blur unseen.

There, before the headlight's stare
stark and barely credible—
> *red wolf running*
> *in the cold blue light, rabbit*
> *limp*
> *almost lost*
> *open-eyed*
> *alert*
> *between the ragged jaws:*

> *life ephemeral*

red in tooth and claw—

he saw,
she saw,

> but left the word

unspoken

Abound

They
bellied up a rock-broke hill
steep, dense with hemlock
and wizened ash

 sharp-turned
         right and up again,
trees closed
a narrow declivity,
              dark as a tunnel,
              pitched like a ski run.
Then came
the dive, the sudden drop,
the sinking
to the bottom
of the sea

legs braced

        pushed straight
        elbows tucked:
        she could not breathe

headlights bounced and rolled
steadily dispersed,
the lurch, the lurch

the head-long and unruly rush
to blackness and the precipice
        a lattice-work
        of creeping vine,
crowded shadow,
withered bracken
threatened
to o'er run the road,
reclaim the right
to things unbounded,
to chaos and collapse of sight.

He gripped the wheel
pumped testosterone and pride
aimed for a small
        white
        circle of light
        at the bottom of the hill
        down,
        down,
        down

to a pounding thump,
a thrust and bounce
a swerve and scrape,

the rising hump
of a frost heave—

a blurred blind sprint
through forbidding trees,
the outstretched reach
of tangled brush,
the smothering intensity,

then out
and free

Breathe, breathe, she thought
the calm relief of open fields
the long-blue gouda-whiteness
              of the river-freezing moon

              eyes closed,
              she shivered
              thighs pressed tight
              and fought the rising fear
              of bedlam:

the red wolf running
in the long dark winter
              night

Loons: the cycle

1

      long April days
he waits

the lonely call unanswered
the worried hoot
the watched return

the risk
   of oil slick
   of mile-long nets
   strangled in a haul of cod
thrown limp for chow
upon a bait bin

but comes the day
the splash and spray
the looked-for guest:

      bills tucked
      they kwuk
      circle and cry
      surface and dive
      two sleek black heads
entwined

their wakes commingled

2

in tall grass near the water's edge,
old nest, flattened by the weight of snow
made new by moss and salvaged sedge
assiduous

and two
soon brown-specked
green-brown eggs

 appear
luminous

3

the wheel of black-backed gull
the turtle's vice-like grip
sea bass teeth
pickerel and pike
skunks and weasel
and hungry coon

amid cries of heron
and hermit thrush
two chicks
abound their mother's back
and peep with life

where danger lurks

4

        the sun
         big, fat,
    golden cat
    implacable

    boils heavy air
    from the languid
and paludal gulf

even dragonflies
refuse to buzz

water soft with movement
misty fog, the chicks
so plump

can scarcely dive,
zig-zag
between their parents' wake
and sail
      the summer's twilight

5

the Bog is red in August,
and grass-pinks and pitcher plants
in fours and fives
are veined so deep

the red is like a pumping blood

6

berries swell and seed heads burst
Queen Anne shimmers in the setting sun
Mosquitoes, black flies subside:

two large and clumsy
dull-grey birds
await
the male

and swim
like chicks to beg

a bounty

7

    first frost has bruised the tender plants
    and brush has turned to brackened brown
    white bark bright yellow birch
abuts blue spruce
and deepened pine

chicks are nearly grown
flight feathers long and straight
whose weight exceeds its strength
who beat and thrash

but cannot fly

8

        geese and ducks
        have flown

hard rains have
blown the leafless trees

high above
two
circle once,

then blink from sight

the sun sinks
behind
a ragged ridge

shell ice rims
the water edge

young loons
remain
bereft
alone

in darkness
swim
long shadows

9

wings along the surface
flap
AND RISE

cushioned by the wild surmise
of lightless air
and boundless sky
trees and rocks and fields
recede

the cold cove ebbs to
silver shine

a small
flat pocket
in the dying light

Madness

I

There came a knock,

> a knock at the door.
> *Strange thing*, she thought,
> living so far from town,
> *to have a sudden knock disrupt the
>   quiet of the day.*

Then came another and another.

> the house shook, recoiled.
> these knocks were not meek nor
>   importunate.
> had no apology to make. No
>   acknowledgement
> of rights, proprietary or otherwise.
> they were blunt, intrusive,
> rocked the ataractic stillness of the
>   house.
> demanded attention.
> craved it.
> Insisted.

A prelude to mayhem, she thought.

perched beneath the transom,
she nudged the curtain of the sidelight
sash—
slowly—just an inch.
And there he was

> Ferocious face unshaven,
> rodent-snouted and predatory—
> gross, vulpine, acquisitive—
> so stark and palpable
> in the harsh October sun,
> it made her gasp (he seemed to
> hear).

she flinched and fell
heart racing,
light-headed,

stared at the shadow
he cast upon the door.

And then, he was gone.

II

the wooden storm door slammed

      the spring wire hummed shut
      heavy boots clomped upon the porch.
      Gone.

Safe: she thought
   and closed her eyes to breathe,
then tiptoed down the hall

at the picture window
she edged forward,
        peeked...

> *And there he was again!*
> So close she almost
> felt hot breath upon her cheek.
> Face pressed against the glass,
> inches from where she stood,
> cupping his eyes with meaty hands
> against the gauze of white curtains,
> the window's blank reflection:
>
> The unaccomodated face.
> The thing itself.
> Smug and complacent.
>
> He snorted,
> gave grunt
> the huge head swiveled back and forth.

She looked for protection:
> a bookend,
> a fire poke,
> a heavy vase.

Chest pounding, throat constricted,
she peeked once more.

> Again, gone.
> Suddenly gone.
> She didn't see him go, but gone.

> She leaned against a chair
> took long breaths
> floating
> buoyant and unreal
> unsure he was there
> at all,
> then certain she saw him smile.

Smile.

Smile vicious and cynical.
An affirmation:

> *This way evil comes.*

Wolf

He was out there.

Waiting.
Watching.

Lurking in the woods.
Worrying his prey.

Each creak the old house made
Each time the burner clicked
Each rattle of a window pane

gave ominous intent
sent her sprawling to the floor,
huddled against
a wall, baseball bat in hand,
doors locked,
shamed by
fear but helpless

The sun yielded slowly
by degrees
to black trees
and daylight failed.

Creeping soundless in the darkened

house, darting past windows,
tiptoeing on stairs,
feeling her way
with utmost care
not to bang a pot or pan,
she prepared the evening meal.

Five-before-six, Tom arrived.
"What's with the lights?" he asked.

Just minutes before, she'd switched
on every one,
in and out,
basement and attic.

"I don't know," she said. "Forgot, I guess."

The Home Stretch

Out the door
while Tom still slept,
running Stones Point Road.
Five miles/forty minutes
to close the cycle.
Time enough before he left.

The hard bright sun
clarified misgiving.
Black crows cawed
and grey squirrels scampered.

The road curved, rolled
up and down. Then the long
flat lonely stretch out to Davis Point.
Misty and Sam (ragged tongues panting)
Joined to Back Cove and barked goodbye.
No loons in sight.

>She heard the water surge, the swell,
>smelled salt. Heron stalked the shallows.
>Gulls and osprey soared.
>The road swerved up.
>The raw green scent of cedar, of sedge,
>of moss-backed rock, sweet clover and
>>bloodroot.

> The sour-mash sap-and-mud smell
> of fresh cut wood.

Left on Cushing Road, past ponds and meadows.
Golden fields with golden flowers, red columbine
and pasture rose, past blonde-mowed fields,
purple lupine and yellow marigold.

She circled the harbor and headed home.

> Maggie met her fair and barking
> galloped up to Olhmeyer's Farm,
> then departed. The Galloways,
> broad and barrel-chested,
> belted black and white, crunched
> the brown-green grass and swished their
> > tails.

> The dirt road narrowed, black and tangled
> pine pushed close. The barrens.
> It was all shadows here, bereft of life.
> She sailed down the long dark hill
> to Dead Pond Road. On both sides,
> the water was oily black and bottomless.

> Rounding the turn,
> she eased into a carefree glide,

The home stretch.

Up Gooseberry Hill, hard by the nubble,
without remorse, toes gripping the road,
running, pushing it. Long strides,
powerful, crisp toe-offs at the crest,
the loop completed. Turned right, back
to Stone's Point. *Safe!* light and elastic,
racing against the mist, the loamy dew.
Anxious to see the rugged angles
of his fresh-shaved face...

but the car was gone,
the house empty,
the door unlocked.
Tom being thoughtful
(though she had her key).

At the back porch steps, she stood
 afraid to enter.

She wanted to mount the stairs
casual as a loaf of bread. Fearless.
Indifferent.
Like Tom would.
"Don't be ridiculous," he'd say and barge
right in.
No vanity. No wild imaginings.

Certain of his body's length.

But she was not Tom.
She was a tiny figure

        and she was afraid.

The First Time He Saw Her

The grass was green
The leaves were red
The band played at half-time.

Small-breasted, round-cheeked,
eyes porcelain and blue
and he, beguiled,
        baffled by her beauty

The women he knew
Had eyes that could deceive
Deny until the bargain's made

But Annie's eyes kept secrets
Instilled, he thought, a duty

                fragile

like a rose

Night

Cover the mirrors
          when he is gone
          when he is gone

Cover the mirrors
          with sheets

all the mirrors
          when he is gone
              gone

fearful
to look in

and forever be lost:

    some secret
    not Him

White in the Moon the Long Road Lies

she sees the house
       at cresting of the hill
       beyond the ridge,
       before the next descent

she sees the house
             cold and empty,
in the dark November night
solitary
forsaken
slightly sinister in the pale blue light.

"We should get a dog," she says.

He smiles and
pulls her close.

The solid Saab
       curls among the empty fields
       elbows into crowded woods
       squeezes out of blackness,

       sprints down
       the Stone's Point Road
       too fast,
       too fast,

she tells him,

brakes
hard to make the turn
the swerve and lurch
and up the long dirt drive
yellow light bouncing
the brown and beaten grass,
the house
the wordless barn

"There!" she cries,
pointing to a wall of darkened trees.

"What?" he asks,
slowing to a crawl.

"Nothing, I suppose."

moonlight now like the world made new
and she
   searching
for a glimpse,
       a hint of something,

something
fixed and certain

in the black and heaving night.

Mirror Image

after Millay

was that her step
in the dustless hall,
her bright laughter
in the silent room—
she that was here
and is here no more

Beloved

witty
willful
but tender
heartfull
soft as a sweet pea

Gone

one clear, quick
November day

ripped asunder
but for remnant of blood:
a scarf, a hat discarded
the offending trace

of semen

tangled in the underbrush
discarded
a thing
nameless
and unaspirated
still clutching
a blue
embattled rose.

    .

and now,
she
left alone
wanders

these cold and vacant rooms
       twinless,
and wonders where
       up?
       down?
not in the broken stump, surely
not in the ground
the clouds

What bitter blood,

And gone *forever*?

she comes no more.

yet, the rooms
are full of her
and her golden laugh;
she lives
and moves about
while earth enfolds
her dreamless dreams

embraces the
nameless
ache, the heartless
light of dawn
the raw new day
the brittle leaves
that scrape and hiss,

a houseless poverty
and

all unbosomed.

Alewives

He woke
to find her sitting

knees bent
hugged tight
slender and elastic
folded like a child.

"So?" he nudged.
"Can't sleep," she said.

A rutting moon cast furtive shadows.
Eyes lurked
       in leafy dark.   and
Up from the water
a sudden cry.
Harsh,
like
       women wailing.
He stirred
to sit,
       alert.

"Gulls," she told him,
hand light to touch
for comfort

on his arm.

    "Gulls? At 3 a.m.?"
but gone before an answer,
bathroom bound
lunged with heavy step.

"Herring in the coves,"
she called.
    "Umph," he mumbled.
"Gulls, crying at night—"
    "What?" he grunted
        the seat upraised.
"—signifies herring in the coves,"

    drowned out by
streaming *man*-pee.
Assertive.
An announcement of self.
    "I wonder what *that* signifies," she thought,
    "Alewives in the anus?"
A secret smile
the seat slammed down
and toilet flushed.

"What?" he asked.
"Gulls, crying at night, means
    herring in the coves."

"Ah." he yawned,
> bounced the bed,
> punched the pillow,
> turned from her.

"Umph," he groaned
> and off to sleep.

She envied that. The quick and simple,
child-like sleep.

·

The gulls kept up their cry,
a savage homesick sound,
and moonlight swelled the curtains—
a cold pale light like ghosts in shadows
and she in darkness
so much apart.
hugged her knees.
Alone.

Listening to slaughter.

Later,
long from her thoughts,
she heard him say,

"It's starting again...
> *Isn't it?"*

The north wind whistled,
whipped stiff brown leaves
in coils that cracked
and hissed at the leaded sill
scratched the cellar door

like a stranger's hand
on the unlocked latch.

Ocean in the Trees

Wind gusted and turned.
Stout grey-and-plump white clouds
against a blue transparent sky. Bright
green grass and dark green
spruce. sugar maple, birch,
and alder, ash all swirl
in gold and red
and yellow.

This day, she thought.
The rise and roll of it.
This day.
The ache and sag.
This day.
The crash and fall.
This day.
The need to embrace it all,
pull it close.
This day.

Rhythm, not collision, she thought.
Harmony. Like the loons.
She wondered how they knew
and when.
Why leave at all? South?
North? How do they know

and with a certainty, unlike herself, their
proper role and place?
No questions. No existential angst.
Just the impulse of flight.
And gone.

"A nation of berry pickers
  if left to you."

Tom knew such things.
The meek were
always vulnerable, but she feared the day
when loons
would come no more.

Forever.

Wind whipped the laundry stiff.
Shirts and blouses
stood right up. The taut clean sheets
 a flag unfurled.

She brushed hair from about her face
and watched as
Homer's wine dark sea
became a sheet of glass and white caps.
"White cats," her sister
                    used to say.

A large black cloud
choked the sun,
clotted it
sent a sudden chill.

She turned.

>*Did someone call?*
>*Was that her name she heard?*

A flash of light, the forest wall foreclosed
there, where the wilderness possessed its

own

a wall impenetrable.

All Knowledge is an Act of Faith

The squall line passed
just before dawn
And now the grass was wet
and the road
black with rain

Scattered clouds sailed low
bilious and white
beleaguered
by a gusting wind

Out the door, she went
feeling clean and scrubbed
Purified,
by the brisk bright air,
settled into
the reassuring thud
of breath and foot

a new day shining

Down the hill
past the pumps at Gushee's Store,
Boats clanking in the bay
as John Snow keyed
The P.O. door

And waved.
The wind pushed
And rattled
Scarred the water white
And blue sky broke
The ragged clouds.
Nuthatch
And chickadee.
Kingfisher
High in the topless sky
Wings wide
Sailed currents
       in pure
       delight
       of flight

Up the hill beyond the bay
Nodded past Julia and Joe Killkelly
White-haired, lean and sparse
Pink-faced, blue-eyed
Of vigorous stride

Near Davis Point
The corner's sharp
She
Picked up speed
Breathing hard

Over the bridge
And to the left and down
Something caught
Her eye
Something like
A mound of fur
Upon a mound of flesh
Something wild and
Naked
Flat buttocks
On the tracks
Below

It caught her breath
Stopped her cold

It was him

The rat-faced man
Pitted hairy flanks
And hairy back now
Facing her

Watch cap on his head

His right arm pumped
Unmistakable
And grotesque

Soundless

In the morning light

Him

    "Afraid," she said
"But there's nothing. . ." he began.
      "Nothing?"

"Christ," he murmured,
      "let go."

      "I have," she said
      and left the room.

      Swift, clean
      Sharp, keen as that,
           the silken ties broke free

Inner Night

she sighed
upon the dashboard's
glow, leaned her head
against the window
gazed an empty moon

waiting for a lover
watching for him
to rise up,

        up, up, Up.

        up
from the puckerbrush
and mist,
not to save her
but to whisper:

that love is more,
that dreams are more

than waiting
for a hero

Holy Trinity

The northbound train to Rockland
Rumbled overhead, below
an amorphous figure
Swung slowly
back and forth

Who shall mourn
The nameless
The naked
And the shameless
Who late in season
Killed the household
Traitor dead
The swollen body
Gross
A watch cap
On its
head
Around his neck
entwined
A carboard sign

"Forgive,"
was all it said.

What she remembered. . .

That though her name was Anna,
He always called her Kate

That he took his coffee
No cream, no sugar.

That she loved

>the flat clean symmetry of his face
>the intricate geometry
>the chiseled grace
>the high cheekbones
>the flat plains

That she loved

>the almost-green eyes
>that looked almost-blue
>whenever the bright sun
>stuffed the cold air tight
>and bounced off the fallen snow

That he never complained
looked afraid
or cried

but for *that* night...

she clicked on a light
and he, sitting in the dark,
wept
       without speaking

"Dad," she called
       but he was gone
       and she alone

              and twin-less.

The Blue Rose

What's wrong, he asked.
She couldn't say.

Her eyes
lifeless
    vacant
    as the moon

not the first time
the long dark ache
progressed
And he
abandoned

You can't live forever
packed in gauze, he told her.

She laughed
    not a real laugh, but something
    hollow and ragged;
She inched close to the door,
gazed out the window
down the empty road

She loved him
and hated herself

for his love.
She lowered her eyes,
yearned to speak
tried to speak
but could not wrap her mouth
around a thing so small
as words

He touched her/
she recoiled

slipped
away

out the door
        and gone

The Remex

bones of sugar maples crossed
the road, underfoot
pale and paper thin
the tattered remnant
fallen slow, the last
to go, yellow leaves
and filtered glow
tunnel of gold. Light,
last light, before
the time of long shadows.

>running the Back Cove
>in mittens and hat,
>scarf trailing behind
>the blink of silver water
>straight ahead

"Anna," she thought she heard.
"Anna," someone called.

She turned, but
no one there.

Near the hunter's cabin
where the creek spills
to the water's edge,

she saw the loons were gone.

Parents just the week before
and now the chicks,
gone
Grown and flown.
All that remained was a

   single
   black
               flight feather
in the clearing near the shore.

The remex

soft and weightless
lonely in the mirrored light

She knelt down
held it in her hands
a perfect thing
fragile and living

The wind began to stir
and blow and yet once more
there came,

"Anna, I'm waiting…"

      a hollow numbness

       a tightness in her chest
       certain, now, she heard
       the name.

"*Anna,*" a male voice called,
       deep, rich baritone
            of melancholy.

"*Anna,*" it called,

      "*Come.*"

She rose slowly to her feet
brushed the feather close
to her lips
and began to run,
legs light, leaping
longing for
the risk
of flight,
yearning

to sail free.

About the Author

Michael Campagnoli taught literature and writing for five years while studying for a PhD. He has worked as a waiter, fisherman, journalist, painter, and short-order cook. He won the New Letters Poetry Award, the All Nations Press Chapbook Award, and The Chiron Review Novella Prize. He can be seen most mornings running somewhere along the coast of Maine with his mongrel dog, Yogi, and Anthony, his equally mongrel son.

Acknowledgments

"White in the Moon," *Claybird*, Spring 2014

"Inner Night," *Spark Anthology*, Spring 2014

"Wolf," *Hawaii Pacific Review*, Spring 2013

"Loons," *Crucible*, Summer, 2011: Vol. 48

"The Long Ride Home," *Ellipsis*, 2011: Vol. 47

"Prelude" and "Alewives" appeared in *The Chaffey Review*, Vol. 6, 2011

"If We're Not A Dream, We're Nothing" appeared in *Weave*, Winter 2010/2011

"Long Shadows," "The Home Stretch," and "Madness," appeared in *Illuminations*, No. 24, Summer 2008

"Loons: *the cycle,*" appeared in a limited edition chapbook, *Loons*, published by Pudding House Publications, September 2008

www.ingramcontent.com/pod-product-compliance
Lightning Source LLC
Chambersburg PA
CBHW021451080526
44588CB00009B/803